101 Things to do (or stop doing)
to give yourself more time RIGHT NOW!

Terry Monaghan

ISBN: 978-0-9916016-0-8 (paperback)
ISBN: 978-0-9916016-1-5 (ebook)

Table of Contents

Part One: At Work

1
Deal with email in batches, 2-3 times a day.

Let's face it. Email will suck up all the time (and more) you have in a day if you don't do something about it. You really do NOT have to jump on every single incoming piece of email as soon as it lands in your inbox. Don't you have actual work to do? So, set up some times you will review everything that has come in. Let people who need to know how you will be handling it. Then shut it off and focus on your own agenda of tasks. It has been said that the email inbox is a perfectly organized collection of every body else's agenda. How about putting your job first?

2

Create a template for your week – what would a perfect week look like?

We like routine, really. We like knowing that we get up at a particular time, eat at a particular time, have certain meetings on regular schedules, etc. Well, you can do the same thing with most of the rest of what makes up your day. Why not figure out your best time for real focused work, and setting that up as an appointment with yourself? You don't have to block out every minute of every day, but try to block regular time for the important stuff. That way you will make progress on those items, rather than be pushed around by the winds of whatever chaos is going on in the moment.

3
Give up multi-tasking

Seriously. Give it up. It doesn't work! It's only an illusion that it enables you to get more done. Time and time again it has been tested, and proven to actually have everything take longer than if each task were done on its own. I get a lot done in a day, and the only multi-tasking I am capable of is listening to music while I am taking a walk. Because it doesn't matter if I miss part of the song! Your work matters. What you are working on matters. The people you are talking to matter. Pay attention. One task at a time really will allow you to get far more done than splitting your attention among many different tasks.

4

Schedule focused blocks of time for different activities.

We've all had the experience of thinking something will take 30 minutes only to discover that it really took us 2 hours from start to finish. Often this is because we are allowing ourselves to be distracted or interrupted in the middle of the task or project. Or, we keep shifting from the phone to the computer to some research to looking for a file to getting a cup of coffee... (insert your own activity here). Try blocking time for phone calls – and make all your calls during that block of time. Or, block time for lunch and actually leave your desk (radical thought, I know). Even a 15 minute block, uninterrupted, will make a difference in your day.

5

Focus on what you do brilliantly, delegate the rest

Imagine this: Your computer hard drive crashes. You hadn't done a backup recently. Everything you need is on that computer. What do you do? Do you spend days researching how to recover lost data (days when you are not doing your own job)? Then, do you attempt to recover your lost data on your own (potentially making it truly unrecoverable)? Or, do you find a computer repair guy quickly and let him/her handle it quickly and thoroughly? Unless your business and expertise is computer repair you have NO business trying to do this yourself. You might actually succeed, but it will take you at least 5 times longer than the expert. That will be hours and hours away from what you actually do to make money. False economies will never save you time (or money).

6

See what can be automated, and automate it

It never ceases to amaze me when I see intelligent individuals doing the same thing over and over, while at the same time complaining that they never have any time. It can take a little time up front to figure out the steps to a process, but once those steps are clearly laid out and the process is clearly defined, much of the time you are spending can be erased. Some examples of what can be automated include: scheduling (using an online scheduling program), order fulfillment, follow up notes or calls, newsletter layout and preparation, some email communication, and many other tasks. The key is to examine the process, see if it can be simply laid out, and then turn it over (either by delegating or by using technology) to someone/something else to be done.

7

Stop doing everyone else's job

At some point you will realize that there are certain tasks that you are really brilliant at – that are your unique gift to the world. We are well served when you focus on doing that! However, along the way, most of you will spend huge amounts of time attempting to do it all. This is such a waste of time! One of the ways entrepreneurs create jobs is by recognizing that they cannot do it all by themselves, and they begin building teams around them. The more you can turn over tasks to a team, the more time you will have to leverage your own unique contribution. Seriously – give up being superwoman/superman. I don't care how well you keep your books, file your papers, or clean your house – if it doesn't add revenue to your business, stop it. Another way to look at this: would you pay someone your salary to do that? If no – for heaven's sake – hire someone else to do it!

8

Don't have your email push through to your smart phone

It used to be that only doctors or emergency responders were set up with pagers that they needed to respond to immediately. And for doctors, that was only when they were on call. What happened? When did we all get so important that we needed to be on call 24 hours a day, 365 days a year? Your email inbox is a perfectly organized collection of everyone else's agenda. (See tip #1.) When did you decide that was more important than working on your own goals? I get it – there are some people you need to respond to with alacrity, and some situations that require your immediate attention. But that most likely only accounts for about 20% at most of what is coming in. If you are going to use email on your smart phone, at least set it up to be pulled into the inbox at your convenience, rather than having each and every message pushed through as it happens. That way, you can skim what has come in to determine if anything is urgent at your convenience. You can also use tools like AwayFind to have specific people or topics pushed through.

9

Turn off noise makers and pop ups for email

By default, we are getting interrupted at least once every 6-8 minutes all day long. And, it takes 10-15 minutes to bring your focus back to what you were doing when you were interrupted. That math just doesn't work. Think about it. You will be interrupted, and you will most likely keep getting interrupted before you can get back to what you were doing (if you even remember what it was). Do you really need to see that pop-up every time you get an incoming email? Do you really need to hear that beep every time something lands in your inbox. Is that more important than what you are working on now? Give yourself a break. Shut it off while you are trying to concentrate. You will not be able to eliminate every interruption, but you can control some of them. Do that.

10

Turn off the phone when you need to concentrate

Have you ever heard of voicemail? The phone is either a tool that will facilitate communication or it is a major interruption in your day. Most desk phones and smart phones have a feature that lets you set it to 'do not disturb' when you need to focus on something. Use it! Let the call go to voicemail. Remember, you can check the voicemail when you have finished what you are working on (or have someone else check it for you). Nothing makes me crazier than being in a meeting with someone (who is paying for my time) and have them stop the action to take a call that really isn't that important. They are wasting their money (they are paying me to sit there) and their time as well.

11

Determine your work hours, and stick to them

Every business has office hours (or store hours, if retail). Why don't you? Why do you feel it is necessary to work all hours of the day and night? Why do you think you need to answer your business phone after hours? Or answer your emails at 11pm? What impact does this have? Impact on you: you have no time off. You are operating as if you are working (or available) 24 hours a day. And you inadvertently train others that you will take their call whenever they call. No boundaries. Impact on your business: you are most likely close to overwhelmed and burnt out. What good are you if you are operating at half speed because you are so worn out? Set your work hours, and stick to them. If you don't honor them, no one else will! And if you must check email late at night, either save your responses to the draft folder to be sent the next work day, or schedule them to be sent during business hours.

12

Plan your work, then work your plan

Take the time to create your plan of action. Schedule the work to be done. Set up regular intervals to review your progress. Correct and adjust as necessary. I am always astonished at those who fail to plan, jump into action, and then wonder what happened when they hit a roadblock. Most say they just don't have time to plan. What they mean is they don't see the value in the planning. Truth is, an hour spent planning can and will save you hours and hours of frustration and wasted effort. Give it a try.

13

If they can't find you, they can't interrupt you.

In the book "No BS Time Management for Entrepreneurs", Dan Kennedy says "If they can't find you, they can't interrupt you." On average, you will be interrupted at least once every 6-8 minutes throughout your day – by the phone, by email, by text, by instant message, by someone stopping by your office. When you really need to focus, make yourself unfindable for a while. Turn off the phone (put it on 'do not disturb' mode), turn off the email, turn off the instant messaging, close the door or leave the office for a while to give yourself some uninterrupted time to think, plan, work. The world will keep spinning without you, and you might actually get something really important done.

14
Respond, rather than react

How much of your day is driven by reaction? The phone rings, you jump. The email dings, you open it. You get an instant message and interrupt what you were doing to read it. You are sorting your email and dive into someone else's agenda. We spend so much energy jumping from one thing to the next with no thought, no consideration and no appreciation of the relative merits of what we are doing. Remember the old adage – count to 10? There's a reason for that. Pausing for a moment, counting to 10 or taking a few breaths with immediately pull you out of reaction, and give you time to consider and respond. That is far less stressful and far more productive.

15

Don't set alerts for everything

It is useful to set some form of alert/alarm for parts of your day. Personally, I set alerts for scheduled appointments and phone calls, to ensure that I am not late or forgetting them. OK, sometimes I also have to set an alarm to remind myself to eat. But I am not setting an alert for every task I have set for my day. Have you ever had an alarm go off and hit the snooze? Or had a computer alert pop up only to snooze/dismiss it – and promptly forget about what it was there for? Too many alerts and alarms become noise and defeat their original purpose. So, determine what are the really important items you need alerts for, and set them. Then honor them when they come up.

16

Take regular breaks

In his book "The Way We're Working Isn't Working," Tony Schwartz points out we work best in pulses. We can focus on something for a period of time, and then we need a period of time to rest. Most studies indicate that we can only focus intently for about 90 minutes tops before we need to take a break. Brendan Burchard advocates taking a short break every hour. I know you think that if you just press on for another 15-20-30 minutes you will get this done, but you are mistaken. If you give yourself periods of time to focus (from 15 to 90 minutes) and regular periods of time to rest, you will get more done than if you just try to muscle through.

17

Set up email rules to automatically sort incoming email

There is this amazing function in most email programs that allows you to set up rules for how your incoming (and sometimes outgoing) email is handled. You can tell the system to automatically move certain messages into certain folders as soon as it arrives. For example, all email where you are cc'd can move into a separate folder. Or, email from certain senders (newsletters, for example) can move into a specific folder. This works well for email you don't need to see as soon as it arrives. Let's say you serve on a volunteer board, for example. Emails for board business don't need to interrupt your normal work day – they could be sorted into a folder to be dealt with at specific times. Try it out! Many of the systems also let you run the rule on your inbox to move anything that is already there into another folder. This will leave you with less in the inbox, and hopefully more time to work.

18

Unsubscribe from newsletters you no longer read

It is dreadfully easy to find yourself on 10-50-100 newsletter lists. If they all publish once a week, that's an extra 10-50-100 emails each week (520 – 2600 – 5200 each year). Let's face it, none of them is important enough to interrupt your job on a daily basis. It's a good practice to re-evaluate the newsletters and ezines you are receiving. Tell the truth – are you reading it? Are you interested in the topic? Are you feeling guilty for NOT reading it? Unsubscribe from those you don't read or are not interested in. I also unsubscribe from those I didn't subscribe to in the first place! Clear out the clutter. Free up the space and energy for something more important.

19

Schedule preparation time for meetings or conferences

Have you ever looked at your calendar and discovered you had a meeting scheduled and you just weren't ready for it? What happened? Most likely, you knew you had work to do to get ready for the meeting, but you didn't set aside the time to do that work. Probably you didn't even look when you were scheduling the meeting itself to make sure you actually had time available to do any preparation required. We often tend to think of a one hour meeting as just taking up one hour of our time, and we schedule it as if that were true. But, how many meetings have you attended as just an observer with no accountability to prepare before or take action after? So, when scheduling meetings, be sure to also immediately schedule the time you need to prepare.

20

Schedule debrief time for meetings or conferences

A client complained once that she was writing proposals at 10:30 at night, which violated her own rules for how she wanted to work. I asked why she didn't have time set aside to debrief (and maybe write proposals) after meetings with prospects. It doesn't have to be the very next block of time, immediately after the meeting – but it should be some time within the next few days, while all the information is still fresh. And I recommend the same thing after attending conferences! Give yourself scheduled time to put things into existence when you get back to your office. This way that pile of contacts you want to follow up with won't get lost in the flood of new work.

21

Regularly give yourself time to think

Have you ever found yourself running so hard and so fast through all the stuff that shows up on your desk that you wonder if you will EVER have time to just think? Well, you won't – at least not unless you schedule that time. And it should be a regular thing on your schedule. Here's a hint – you rarely think when you are sitting in front of a computer. Get up, get out, go somewhere else. Give your brain a chance to work!

22

Delegate as much as you can

Just because something needs to be done doesn't mean YOU need to be the one doing it! I suspect this is a radical thought for a few of you, and some others of you are now hyperventilating! But really, ask yourself "Am I the one who is uniquely qualified to do this?" Another great question is "Would I pay someone what I get paid to do this?" If the answer to either question is no, then find someone else to take on the task, and move on.

23

Do regular computer backups

You only need to have your hard drive crash once to realize how much time and sanity you will save if you set your computer up for regular backups. Trust me on this – don't wait till it's too late! It doesn't matter if you use an external hard drive or an online service – get it set up and let it run.

24
Have a clear process for handling your email

Let's face it – we are all drowning in email. We've gone from spending an average of 15 hours a week (in 2006) on the inbox to receiving in excess of 250 pages a day (in 2012), and it isn't going to stop anytime soon! What's missing is a process for dealing with what comes in. Here's a hint – use your inbox to SORT rather than STORE. That way, you can identify and move each piece to the next stage very quickly, grouping like items with like.

25
Debrief your day

Take a few minutes at the end of each day to review what you worked on, what got accomplished, what still needs to be done. Make a note in the appropriate places about calls to make, messages to return and other action items requiring your attention. This will allow you to leave the office behind when you leave the office for the day, without worrying about the proverbial other shoe dropping in your absence.

26

Review the next day's agenda at the end of the day

Set aside some time at the end of your workday to glance over what is coming up in your schedule. Review tomorrow's agenda. Make notes of anything you need to gather together to make the day run smoothly. If you will be having meetings outside of the office, put what you need to bring with you into your briefcase now. Don't wait till tomorrow, when you may be rushing around! What needs to be added to your plan for tomorrow? What's been moved or removed?

27

Get very clear about your strategy – what is the point of what you are doing?

Have you ever looked at your to do list and had the thought "what is all of this about?" When your task list occurs like an endless list of stuff to do, it is almost certainly because you have lost sight of the bigger picture. The actions on your schedule (hopefully) should relate to the fulfillment of goals you are actively working on. So, each task brings you one step closer to achieving the goal. You may need to take time and step back to give yourself the broader view of what you're actually doing. It's very hard to see the field when you are looking at it from the perspective of the field mouse. The owl has a wider view by virtue of a different perspective. Give yourself that perspective before you dive back into the individual tasks.

28

Set up your work space to work!

I have a theory. Your work space is either set up in such a way as to invite you in and support you in what you are doing, or it is somewhere else on the spectrum up to and including compelling you to run screaming from the building! It has been documented that many of us will spend at least one hour a day looking for things. If you set up your office (or wherever you work) to work FOR you (rather than AGAINST you), you can eliminate most of that time. What you need will be where you need it when you need it. Please note, this does NOT mean a huge amorphous pile on your desk! You may be able to reach into the pile and pull out just the piece of paper you are looking for, but if anyone else touches the pile (or if gravity attacks and the pile cascades over) you are in real trouble. Take some time to figure out what you need for your space to be truly functional, and make a plan to get your space in shape. (Hint: There are people who will help with this. You don't have to do it on your own.)

29

Order office supplies online

I love going to the office supply store. OK, I am strange, but I know I'm not the only one. Where others love wandering through the mall window shopping the newest fashions, I love wandering through the office supply store looking at all the cool tools and supplies available. However, wandering through the office supply store is NOT a great use of my most productive time. So, I have created various favorite supply lists on my store's website. When I need to replace something I've run out of, it only takes a moment to order it online. And then they deliver it right to my door! This also helps me keep my budget in line, I must admit. I do drop into the store just to wander around from time to time (and always find something I really need), but for the bulk of my purchases, I order online.

30

Try meeting by phone or Skype or videoconference vs. in person

A client was nearly tearing her hair out during a private scheduling workshop for her team. The problem was (she said) she had several different contractors/consultants she was managing and when she needed to meet with them, she was driving all over the area, spending huge chunks of time in traffic rather than working. Even if she stacked those meetings on one day, she would still spend nearly half of the day driving from one place to the other. I looked at her and asked why she wasn't using one of the video conferencing tools available for those face to face meetings. I know she needed to actually meet with them in person occasionally, but for the bulk of the other meetings, video conference would work just fine. And it would give her back that half day, not to mention eliminate the stress of the traffic.

31

Block out time to focus

Let's face it, most of us don't take the time to focus when we really need to. We try to wedge things in to available moments in time, which often results in us switching from task to task to task throughout the day, without finishing anything. Give yourself the luxury of blocks of time to focus on one thing and one thing only. Even if it is only for 15 minutes! You will be amazed at what you can get done in just 15 minutes when you let yourself focus on it. Remember, if you do nothing, by default you will be interrupted at least once every six minutes, all day long. That is the path to frustration.

32

Use as much technology as you are comfortable with

There are some really great tools available to support you in your work. Laptops, desktops, tablets, smart phones, etc., all can combine to help you get things done faster and more efficiently than ever before. But the technology has to work for you. It is, after all, just a tool. You don't have to do email on your smart phone just because that feature is available, for example. Unless it is useful to you, feel free to ignore it. Here's an example. I've been thinking it would be cool to have an iPad. I have a MacBook Pro and an iPhone, and I do love the Apple products. However, when I really looked at what I would use an iPad for, I discovered (at least for now) that it really wouldn't add to my productivity. In fact, it would just add more stuff I had to take with me on business trips. Some of the features and functions I would want to use are not currently available, and others are just as available on my iPhone and my laptop. So, that piece of technology isn't making it onto my list right now. However, I have some clients who have and use and LOVE their iPad. It makes what they do out in the field so much easier and is so much easier to carry around than their laptop! What makes sense to you?

33

Create a weekly magic list – who will you reach out to? What will you create?

If you are in sales (and if you own the business, you are in sales), you have to talk to people all the time. Every day, every week, every month you have to pick up the phone and make calls. You can complain about it as much as you like, but you still have to make those calls. So, since complaining isn't going to get rid of them, why not try something different? Sit quietly at the beginning of the week and ask yourself who you want to talk to in the coming week. Who do you need to call back? Who haven't you checked in with lately? Who did you meet recently? Which of your clients have birthdays, anniversaries or other events coming up? If you are using some form of Customer Relationship Management system, it may have some reports you can use to generate your list of people to call. I've used this process for years. It's astonishing what can happen. Just the routine of making the calls starts things moving.

34

One hour a day marketing (every single day) will have a HUGE impact

If you really want to eliminate that feast or famine cycle – take this on! You know what I am talking about: You have NO business in the pipeline, so you throw yourself into marketing like a crazy person. Guess what? You generate business! Yay! But, now you are just too busy to keep up with the marketing. After all, you have all this work to get done! Then you finish that work, and you have NO business in the pipeline and the cycle starts all over again. Let's face it – business development is the #1 job we have. What can you put in place to make sure that you are taking action to keep your pipeline filled every single day? My personal favorite: Make 3-5 calls every morning to former clients, colleagues, prospects. Leave messages if you have to, but make the calls. How about creating a steady flow of business? Or, even so much business that you have to grow and expand?

35

Set aside a regular time for follow up

You've met all these great people – in person at events, online through social media, or via email introductions from others. You know you have to follow up with them, and it had better be quickly! But you are too busy right now – your schedule is just packed. So, you set those cards aside telling yourself you will follow up 'soon' – just as soon as you finish this one thing. Then days go by, or weeks or months, and you find the card/email again and kick yourself for not following up before now. And now it is too late. What if you just had one appointment a week in your calendar marked for follow up activities? And what if, during that one appointment a week which has been scheduled, you made your follow up calls, wrote your notes, etc.? I promise you, scheduling one hour (or even just 30 minutes) in your calendar on a regular basis will save you tons of time – and will probably add to your bottom line!

36

Have a lawyer review your contracts

You get what you pay for. We've all heard that, right? But how often have you told yourself "I can't afford that right now", and besides, I trust that person, I'm sure there isn't anything in the contract I am going to sign that could cause trouble… It's a really good idea (really, really good idea) to have an attorney draw up your contracts – the ones you ask other people to sign. And it is also a really, really good idea to have an attorney review any contract you are about to sign. Terms of contracts are written to protect the person presenting the contract. And, did you know, you can ask to modify terms? Well, you won't get the chance if you don't read the contract! And since I know you are busy, you may as well have someone who knows what to look for read it for you!

37
Take a short break every hour

I know you are too busy to do this, and you just have too many things you need to do, and I can't really be serious, but I am! Set a timer if you have to. Take a break. Get up for 5 minutes and walk around. Or just stop and take five deep breaths. You will get more done, I promise!

38

Focus on one thing at a time

I never really understood why people brag about their ability to multitask. They really can't do it. No one can. Brain science indicates that at best we can do two things – and one half of our brain will keep track of one thing while the other keeps track of the other. But add in a third thing and all best are off! Productivity studies have demonstrated that when you attempt to multi task everyone takes longer. Yes, every single ting takes longer to do. So stop it. Do one thing. Finish it. Then do the next thing.

39
Set a timer

If you tend to get lost down various rabbit holes, or lose track of time in general, then set a timer. Set a timer to remind you to tke a break. Set a timer to remind you when you have to stop one activity to get ready for another. Set a timer when you want to goof off, so you don't lose the whole day when you just meant to give yourself a brief break.

40

Give up being a perfectionist

How many times have you NOT finished something because you didn't get it perfect? You heard it had to be done a specific way, but you just didn't do it that way, so obviously it wasn't done the right way, so what is the point? Do you know how exhausting that is? Have you ever wondered how much energy and time you were wasting trying to get something to be perfect? What is perfect, anyway? Usually, some way OTHER than the way we are doing it. Give yourself a break. See if just getting it done will make a difference. Sometimes good is good enough. And done is better than not done!

41

De-clutter your office

One of the reasons many of us get overwhelmed is the sheer volume of stuff that surrounds us. It has been said that the average person spends up to one hour a day looking for things. That adds up to 6-8 weeks out of every year – just looking for stuff! I don't know about you, but I can tolerate a certain amount of clutter and disorder. But sometimes that clutter and disorder gets out of hand! One piece of paper out of place doesn't seem so bad, but when that one piece calls hundreds of his little friends, and they call their friends, all of a sudden (it seems) your tidy pile is a huge cascade. Trust me, it doesn't happen over night. When it does happen, get help. Declutter. Tackle one pile at a time. Remember, it didn't happen overnight, and it won't be resolved overnight. But, if you take on a bit at a time you will get it done. And then you will discover you have more energy for what really matters to you.

42

Don't print that if you don't really need a hard copy!

I remember one colleague who printed out every single email they received, and every single document. So they not only had an overflowing digital inbox, they had an overflowing physical inbox too. I get it. Some people actually need to have the piece of paper in their hands. But I challenge you to be ruthless with yourself. Do you really need a hard copy? Or do you just need a reliable place for the digital copy? Do your bit to save a tree. (And if you need a reminder, read the post about decluttering your office!)

43

Keep an extra printer cartridge and an extra ream of paper

Has this ever happened to you? You are head down, focused, working on a major project. You get the project done, and go to print it out, only to have the ink run out, or the paper run out? Or is that just me? Now you have to stop every thing and go to the store to get ink and/or paper! And you don't have TIME for this today! And you are pressed right up against that major deadline, and this lack of supplies could jeopardize the whole thing! Here's a suggestion: Always order an extra ream of paper and an extra cartridge. (Or an extra box of paper if you have the room for it.) Then, when you use the next to last one – REORDER it immediately! Sometimes I think it is a little bit like discovering you are out of TP after you have done your business. Aggravating and unnecessary with a little bit of planning and forethought.

44

Build a favorite items list at your online office supply site, and use it

Most of us are creatures of habit. We always buy the same things. The same paper, the same pens, the same ink, the same toner, the same calendars, the same cards. You get the point. Full disclosure – office supply stores are some of my favorite places to wander around. I think it is the way some women feel about shoe shopping. However, I can spend a long time wandering, and I usually don't have time for that – especially if I am going to the store because I have run out of something I need right away! So, I do most of my ordering of supplies online. Every single site I use has a feature that lets you build your list of favorite items. Which makes reordering stuff very quick and easy. I don't want to search the website for the specific paper I prefer every time I go to the website! I want to get on, place my order, pay for it, and get off!

45

Do your single most important task first each day

Let's face it. You took the time to plan your day. You know what really needs to get done. How often have you walked into your office and been sidetracked by the email or phone message you just got – taking you off on some tangent that had absolutely nothing to do with you what you really needed to get done! Try doing your most important thing FIRST – before you move on to the emergency du jour.

46

Facebook will wait

I know, I know – I love Facebook too! It's such fun to see what people I care about are up to. However, it is also far too easy to spend way too much time scrolling through everyone's comments and updates. Try having your Facebook time be a reward for the accomplishment of a task. That is – get the task done, produce the result, and then give yourself a little break. Remember – set a timer so you don't get lost.

47

Voicemail is there for a reason, use it

Have you even called someone, gotten their voicemail, and just left a message that said, "Hi, it's me. Call me?" Did you ever get that kind of message? What a waste of time! Now, I am supposed to call you to find out why you were calling and then perhaps take some action. How about leaving a complete message – including the reason for the call and perhaps even what the next step might be or what actions you are looking for? That way, when I call back I can move the whole conversation forward.

48

Let your incoming calls go to voicemail, too

Here you are – head down, really focusing on some important piece of work. Things are going well, you are really flying through this project. And then, the phone rings. And you answer it! Which leads to a 10 minute conversation that has nothing to do with what you were working on, and another 20 minutes while you look for or provide whatever the caller wanted. Now, where were you on the project? You do remember the project, right? Oh, yes – here it is! But you've forgotten exactly where you were, so now you have to review it all over again to get your head back into that game. Here's a radical thought: Turn off the ringer on your phone when you need to focus! Or use the Do Not Disturb function on the phone. Don't give that piece of machinery the power to interrupt. Let the call go to voicemail. You can check it when you finish up that piece you were concentrating on…

49

Be careful how often you play phone tag

How much time have you lost in playing phone tag? I think it is related to the tip about how to use voicemail – leave complete messages. If the message is "Call me" – and I have to call you to even find out what you want in the first place, that takes time! But, if you leave a complete message, and the other person can return the call with the information you need, you have saved both of you precious time. My rule of thumb is to leave one or two messages and then follow up with an email if I still haven't heard back. This works well for me, and is worth a try.

50

Take notes on client calls

Actually, that should be: take notes on all calls. Have you ever been on a call with a client, prospect, friend or family member, and agreed to take some action, only to forget about it as soon as you hang up the phone? Get in the habit of taking notes when you are on the phone! I keep a small notebook right next to my phone on the desk, and each day, I put the date on top of a new page, and use it to take notes throughout the day. Any action items get captured there, and then put into the schedule at the end of the day when I review all my notes. I also transfer notes from client calls into my client records. This is one of the key suggestions to get more done without dropping anything through the cracks. And, it is a great use for all those notebooks you get at conferences…

Part Two: At Home

51

Open snail mail once a week

I don't know about you, but much of what I receive in the mail doesn't require me to stop whatever I am doing in the moment to deal with it. So, I have established a practice of bringing all my mail to one place (for me, that is a basket on a table). Then, once a week, I take the basket and open and sort out what has arrived. Since I have already disposed of junk mail, this task takes me about 5 minutes a week and when I am done, the filing is ready, the bills are in their own folder, and the magazines are in the rack. The rest of the paper (envelopes, catalogs, inserts) has been recycled or shredded.

52
Put junk mail into recycling immediately

I love the place I live! They have put recycle bins down by the mailboxes. So, once I pull the mail out of my mailbox, I can immediately recycle the junk mail, and it doesn't even make it into my home to be dealt with later. You may want to put a recycle bin right near where you sort your mail, so that you can just dump stuff as you sort.

53

Do your grocery shopping online

I like to eat. And I like to eat healthy. But what I don't like to do is take time out of my day to go to the grocery store, fill up a cart, load up the car, bring it home, unpack it all and put it all away. And I especially dislike doing all that on the weekend, when everyone else is trying to do the same thing. So, I do my grocery shopping online. My favorite stores have this feature. I can build my list of staple items, and regular items. I can still see all the store specials. And for the enormous sum of under $10, I can have someone else take it all off the shelves, pack it up and deliver it right to my door! No lines. No crowds. And tons of time saved: 5 minutes placing order, maybe 10 minutes putting it all away, vs. 60-90 minutes round trip to the store. Give it a try!

54

Keep your keys / glasses / sunglasses / purse / briefcase in one consistent place

Statistics indicate that we are spending an hour a day, every single day, looking for things. That adds up to 6 to 8 weeks every year, and years over your lifetime. You will save much of that time if you have a specific place to keep keys, glasses, purses, briefcases, cell phones, etc. You may end up spending the time looking for something else, but you will always know where your keys are!

55

Get your regular household items delivered

It is a pain in the butt going to the store and finding half of your cart filled with cat litter, toilet paper, paper towels, shampoo – all the things you need, you use, but you don't buy every week. How about putting them on a list with a service like Drugstore.com or Soap.com or even Amazon.com? Then, when you need to reorder, you can just go online, put in the order, and have those bulky items delivered right to your door!

56

Get your groceries delivered

And while I'm on the topic of grocery shopping – please! How much time do you spend getting ready to go, going, shopping, coming home, unpacking and putting it all away? And if you have kids, it can be a monumental task just getting them ready to go with you. Never mind the fact that you could do it much faster on your own... Again, try one of the online services where you can order your groceries, take advantage of the weekly specials, and have someone else pack it up and deliver it to you? But I want to pick out my OWN produce! Yes, I can hear you say that. And I used to feel the same way. Until I gave it a try, and discovered that the produce delivered was fresher than what was in the store! End of discussion. Frankly $8 per delivery is worth it to save myself more than an hour. And it is very budget friendly, too.

57

Hire someone to run your errands

Bills need to go to the post office, this pile of clothes to the dry cleaners, that pile to the tailor, these bags need to be returned to that store, and those checks have GOT to get to the bank. Oh, and somewhere in there you need to pick up that prescription, take the car in for an oil change, and maybe a car wash. And you work full time. Is it any wonder our lists of what has to get done follow us around like two year olds: mom, mom, mom, mommy, mom… Imagine having someone you could call and give all those errands to! Trust me, you can find someone who would be happy to do all that for you for just a few bucks (or a trade of time). How much time would you gain back if all of that were done for you?

58

Hire someone to clean your house

Face it, we all want a clean, orderly home. Someplace we can relax and live. We don't want to be filled with anxiety at the thought of someone coming in and finding out how we RE-ALLY live. I am quite capable of cleaning my home. I even have been known to do a good job of it. But, frankly, I would rather spend that time working with clients, playing with friends, or chilling with a great book and a nice wine. So, having someone else take care of the heavy cleaning every month (every other week, every week, whatever) is a real joy. And a real time saver! A pro does it better than you do, and faster. You deserve it.

59

Hire someone to do your laundry

This never goes away. Ever. Seems like there is always laundry to do. It either needs to be washed, dried, folded, ironed, or put away. And I am sure I am not the only person who has dressed from the laundry basket of clean clothes just because I haven't gotten around to putting them away. I am also not the only person who has realized I have run out of clean undies! Running to the store to buy new undies just gets old after a while! It was a real gift when I had someone take care of my laundry for me. Remember back to when you were a child and clean clothes just magically appeared? Yes, it is like that. But now you are old enough to appreciate it. Add up how much time you are doing laundry (sorting, washing, drying, ironing, folding, putting away), and don't forget to add in the time you are worrying about it or apologizing for it. What would it be worth to you to have that time back?

60

Put your bills on automatic payments

Am I the only one who forgot to pay a bill because I thought I would rather write checks and had every intention of doing it on a specific day each month, but then got distracted and forgot? I hate those late fees, and wondering what is wrong (with me) that I can't remember such a simple thing! Well, putting my regular bills on automatic payment has put an end to all of that! No more late fees. No more forgotten payments. No more missed deadlines. Easy. Simple. Painless. Oh, and most importantly, done on time!

61

Get your will done!

Seriously. If you are married, get your will done. If you are single, get your will done. If you are young, get your will done. If you are older, get your will done. Trust me, if you don't do your own will, your state of residence already has plans for anything you leave behind. And while those plans may mirror your intentions (but not always), the process will take much longer and be much more stressful for whoever has to sort out the details. Get it done already.

62

Get your advanced medical directive done

God forbid, you find yourself in a situation where someone else needs to make medical decisions on your behalf. If you have taken the time to do the advanced medical directive, you have already said who can do that. Otherwise, the courts will be making the decisions – and the courts don't know what you want! And, by the way, if you have done this, but it was prior to 2010, you need to have it reviewed. The laws changed, and your document might not be in compliance with the new laws!

63

Get a durable power of attorney done

Similarly to the prior tip – you need to spell out exactly who can make decisions and act on your behalf if you ever find yourself in a situation where you are unable to act for yourself. Your bills still need to be paid. Who is going to do that? Who is going to be empowered to take all the appropriate actions for you? Again, if this isn't done by you – the courts will be the ones deciding, and that takes time and money. And doesn't always go the way you would want.

64

Get rid of (give away / donate) what you don't use or don't need

We all have too much stuff. We have so much stuff that some of it is crammed into closets, attics, basements, storage lockers. We don't even remember what we have! Consider selling or donating your excess stuff. I go through all my clothes twice a year and discard or donate what I don't wear anymore. I also go through my books periodically and do the same. It feels good to give the stuff to organizations or to people who will give it more life and will love and use it. It also makes room for new stuff to come in.

65

Plan your meals

I don't know about you, but when I am hungry I really don't want to have to think about what I want to eat. And sometimes I really don't want to prepare anything either. So, I found that planning my meals in advance keeps me on the right track. I don't end up eating out or going for fast food just because I am tired. So, set aside a little bit of time to plan out your meals for the week, and save yourself a lot of time at mealtime all week long.

66

Do all (or most) of your meal prep and cooking once a week

Obviously, this is related to the prior tip! If you are going to take the time to prepare a meal, why not prepare several at once. It doesn't take any longer, and the time saving can really add up over your week. Even if all you do is make a double batch of your favorite dish. You end up with one meal for now and one for later. And you aren't doing prep, cooking, clean-up every single say.

67

Send that pile of mending to the tailor

I can't be the only person who has clothes I can't wear right now because (a) it needs a button resewn, or (b) it needs to be taken in or let out, or (c) the hem is coming down. And I have really good intentions about doing that mending. But, in reality, it isn't going to happen! Find a local tailor and let them take care of this for you. You will get the mending done, and while you will pay a bit for that, you will save all the time you spend worrying about what you aren't doing. And, bonus, you will be able to wear your clothes!

Part Three: In Life

68
Schedule regular goof off time

You need regular down time. You need regular rest time. And often you think you will fit it in as soon as you finish this particular project. But, that never seems to happen, does it? It doesn't fit in, and pretty soon you have gone weeks without any time to just goof off. So, you have to schedule it. Mark that time in your calendar. Honor it. Even if you only manage one hour to completely unplug, do it! It's a start and will make a difference. You will come back to everything else refreshed.

69

Schedule all regular medical appointments at once (for the whole year)

You know you have your annual physical and any associated tests. You know you have to see the dentist twice a year, and the eye doctor as well. Why not schedule them way in advance, and schedule the whole year. This gives you the opportunity to choose days and times that really work for you, rather than being at the mercy of an already full schedule (yours or the doctor's).

70

Schedule all personal care appointments for the year at once

Ladies (and gents), let's face it. We really do need to take care of our hair on a regular basis. If you know you should get your hair cut/trimmed/colored every six weeks, why not schedule all of your appointments at once? No one said you had to make a separate call for each appointment! As with scheduling your doctor appointments, this gives you the opportunity to find days and times that really work for you, rather than having to fit yourself into someone else's schedule. This also applies to any other personal care appointment you need: massage, manicure, facial, etc.

71

Make a map of your year (once a year) – it gives a different perspective

Many of us have a really skewed idea of what our year looks like. This leaves us frustrated and frazzled sometimes when a holiday or other event comes barreling down on us. It is a great exercise to take a year at a glance calendar and think through your upcoming year. This doesn't need to be in a lot of detail, but sketching in the broad strokes will really give you a different perspective on your year. I keep a year at a glance up where I can see it, too. It let's me plan things appropriately and see where I may have bottlenecks with my time. When you work this way, you will block out travel, vacations, time off, family events, and big projects – giving you a great overview of what you have to deal with.

72

Focus on what is important regularly

Far too often, our time and attention is completely taken up with whatever crisis is in front of us. And it doesn't have to be a crisis, it could just be the mundane routine of our daily lives. We lose track of what is important – what we are creating, why we are doing what we are doing in the first place. Set aside some time periodically to reconnect with your dreams and goals. It doesn't need to be every week, and it doesn't need to be a huge amount of time, but is does deserve regular attention! Why will this save you time? Well, when you regularly review what's important, you are less likely to find yourself chasing down rabbit holes that take you off track.

73

Schedule at least one full day off every week

Don't just schedule it, take it! Time off is important. It's vital. It's not negotiable. Figure it out. You have to rest, and you need and deserve at least one whole day. This doesn't mean you do chores that day either! This is a day of rest. I know when you are crazy busy and have a 35 page list of chores and projects to do that this sounds like an impossible idea. But trust me, you will have more energy and enthusiasm for everything that makes up your life when you have had some rest.

74

Take your vacation

Schedule it when you do your year at a glance. Plan it out. Take it. Schedule at least a week at a time, and more if you can swing it. No work allowed on the vacation. Seriously. None. Plan your turnover at work so you can completely unplug and enjoy your time off.

75

Keep ONE calendar (you have ONE life)

Have you ever scheduled something for work and then discovered that you completely forgot some important family event that is happening at the same time? The event doesn't even have to involve you, but something about the event requires your attention, and you now have two things to do in the same bit of time. How does this happen? Too often you will have a work calendar, a personal calendar, and a family calendar. If you don't figure out how to have these overlap so you can see potential conflicts, you will continue to find yourself stressed out and overcommitted. Luckily, technology has some answers. You can easily set up individual calendars using Google Calendar (just one example) that allow you to overlap the different calendars to find potential conflicts or problems before they balloon out of control.

76

Keep a notebook handy for dumping your mind

Brain studies have shown that if you try to keep things in memory (like your to do lists), your brain keeps trying to work on the problem until it is resolved. This is great if it is a problem you need to deal with right now, but if your list contains items for "someday" or "later" or "next year", do you really want to use up that space now? Get it out of your head and into a notebook or computer file. That way (1) you will actually remember it, since the paper is more reliable than you are, and (2) you will give your brain a chance to relax. Or am I the only one who had thoughts chasing themselves around my mind like deranged hamsters?

77

Keep a notebook handy for notes during the day

OK, this one is related to the last one. Things just happen way too fast all day long to rely on your memory! How many times have you had a thought about something you needed to do, and figured you would remember it, only to discover hours (or days) later than you, in fact, forgot? Am I the only one who has gone into a store for just one thing that I needed, only to walk out with a bag full of other things and NOT the one thing I went in for? Get in the habit of carrying around a little notebook and take notes through the day. You can review the notebook at the end of the day to see if anything needs action. I date my notebooks, and keep one on my desk all day to jot phone numbers, ideas, tasks, etc.

78

Getting from place to place takes time, plan for it

I live in the Washington, DC area. The joke here is the only thing we really need for a huge traffic jam is a day that ends in "Y". Add in any kind of weather (sun, rain, snow) and all bets are off! And still, I can't believe how many people use "traffic" as a reason for being late. Just because you could, theoretically, get from Alexandria to Tysons Corner in 15 minutes (at 3:30 am on a Tuesday), doesn't mean you should PLAN on getting there in 15 minutes! It's much less stressful to plan for the trip to take much longer. Then, if it doesn't, you are golden, and if it does, you are still on time. You could use that extra time (when you actually arrive early) to make some calls, read a report or a book, or just breathe.

79

Use an e-reader – you can read while you are waiting for something else

See Traffic. It's small, it's portable, you can get books, magazines, newspapers, etc. One of my complaints is I just don't seem to get the time to read that I used to! But with the e-reader on my smart phone or laptop, I had to give up that excuse! Now, I can read whenever I have a few minutes between other things. And it keeps track of where I left off!

80

Don't let other people's emergencies distract you

I used to have a little cartoon in my office that showed a neat and tidy desk, with a wall clock showing 5:10pm. The caption was "lack of planning on your part does not constitute an emergency on mine." But, really, how often are you swept up in someone else's drama? It's exhausting – most especially when it is NOT really an emergency! Getting hit by a car is an emergency. Don't get me wrong, I am not advocating that you ignore them. But, keep your priorities straight! Don't let your desire to help someone out get in the way of accomplishing YOUR goals.

81

Take care of yourself first

You remember that announcement we have all heard on the airplane? The one about, in the event of an emergency, put your own oxygen mask on first, then help those around you? Well there is a reason for that! We are so used to looking out for everyone else (especially women), and putting ourselves last, that we are in real danger of harming ourselves. If you are the one taking care of everyone around you, what do you think is going to happen when you need taking care of? Most likely, no one will be coming to your rescue. It is not selfish to take care of yourself first. It is very selfish to work yourself to the point of exhaustion. I get it, you want to give of yourself. But if you don't also take care of yourself, you will have nothing left to give.

82

Build your life support team

Several years ago I was attending a business seminar where the leader talked about building a life support team. What a great concept! Being curious, I asked her what would be the first three positions to consider. Here's what she recommended. (1) Find a personal assistant – someone who can run errands for you. (2) Get someone to clean your house. (3) Hire someone to handle your bookkeeping. And for families, her suggestion included (4) get help with the kids! I can hear you screaming now. But consider, if you had someone who could run errands for you or wait for the cable guy, how much more could you get done in that time? Most of us could surely generate enough to cover the small cost. I know my first assistant paid for herself in the time she saved me!

83

Be sure to set aside time for your family

Too often we get so busy doing what we are doing that we lose sight of why we are doing it in the first place. What good is building an empire if there is no one there to celebrate with you? Take time to nurture those relationships! You will come back to work refreshed and renewed and with clear priorities.

84

Do something you love to do

Personally, I kind of like the idea of a bucket list – a list of things you want to do before you die. Why not make sure that there is something in each day or each week that feeds your soul? Taking time away from the day to day routine is one of the best things you can do for your productivity. And when you spend that time doing something you love, you bring that enthusiasm back with you.

85

Hire someone to do your taxes (save you time AND money)

As often as the tax code is changed, and as confusing as even the simplest forms can be, investing in a pro is a very smart way to go. Yes, it will save you time, but more importantly, it will ultimately save you money. A pro will make sure you take all the deductions you are entitled to. A pro can minimize the mistakes you might make yourself. I have never regretted the money I pay my accountant to make sure my books are straight and my taxes are done right. Peace of mind is a wonderful thing.

86

Find a dry cleaner who will pick up and deliver

I live in a building that has a dry cleaner in the market on the property. Sometimes I even remember to take my dry cleaning down to drop it off. But then I will keep forgetting to pick it up! I am not scatter-brained, but I am usually focused on other things. Having someone pick up my dry cleaning and bring it back to me has been a real treat! And almost no additional cost! Having the right clothes at the right time, clean and pressed = priceless!

87

Use a personal shopper

Ok, full disclosure here. I am not a shopper. I don't like wandering around stores seeing what's there, what's new or cool or different. I would rather go in, grab what I am specifically looking for, and get out as fast as I can. So, when I discovered that stores have personal shoppers on staff, I was very excited. Now, when I need to revamp my wardrobe, I call up and make an appointment with the personal shopper. She grabs things from all over the store and gathers them in one place for me. I can now go in at the scheduled time, try on whatever she has already gathered, make my selections and leave! And I don't have to pay for her services! It's a real time and money saver.

88
Get a personal assistant

I know this sounds like a fantasy, but imagine if you had someone you could turn over a bunch of tasks to, who would actually get them done? There are many ways to do this, one of which is using one of many concierge services to run your errands. When I asked a mentor who suggested building a life support team who she considered essential – personal assistant was the first role she mentioned. You can really get creative here. This is not a full time position, so you could find someone who is available one hour a day, or a few hours a week – whatever you do, just give it a try. You will wonder how you ever lived without one.

89

The post office will pick up your packages!

With cutbacks, work hours and everything else, just getting to
the post office can be a real pain. And once you get there, you
either have to figure out their automated system (assuming it
is working), or wait in line. Well, guess what? The post office
will actually come and pick up your packages! Yes, you read
that right. They will come to your door and pick them up and
take them away. Now, why aren't you using that service?

90
Give up your to-do list

You have a 35 page, single spaced, list of things you want to do, think you should do, or plan to do some day. While that may work for some people, for most it is just overwhelming! And truth be told, you don't really have a 35 page to do list. That might be your master list of all the projects or activities you want to get to, but the to do list is just what you are going to do today. Having said that, how many of you have put 15 items on today's list, only to finish one of those items? And then you feel bad and frustrated and overwhelmed (again). What if, instead of doing a to do list, you sat down and planned out your day – in time – and wrote in what you were going to do and exactly when you were going to do that? This would give you a far more powerful (and realistic) view of your day and what was going to actually get done. And, you can also refer back to some of my earlier tips, and delegate a bunch of your tasks to someone else.

91

If it isn't scheduled in time, it isn't happening!

Too often, I think, we approach quite a lot of what we have to do with the thought "I'll fit that in somewhere." How often does that really work? More often than not, I assert, it doesn't work at all! We don't get things done, and then we wonder why? Everything we have to do takes time to be done. Why do you suppose we ignore that when we are making our lists? One of the most interesting processes for managing the day I read about had an exercise where you were instructed to list all the things you were going to do, and put next to each item exactly how long it would take to do the task. Then, of course, you had to confront the reality of the day and see that, most of the time, you were trying to fit 10 hours of work into a five hour slot. You can imagine how that goes. I encourage you to try that out for yourself – see what happens when you actually put only 1 hour of work into that 1 hour slot. And don't forget to include driving from point A to point B if the task requires it! Things might get done from your list, but the chances increase dramatically when you schedule exactly when you are going to do them!

92

Schedule regular activities for the same day/time each week

We love routines! We actually thrive on routine. All the business books talking about decision fatigue share the view that the more routine we can build into our days, the more productive we can be. To look at it from another point of view – imagine how chaotic life would be if work or school had different hours every day? One day, you work from 9 to 5, the next from 2 to 7, and the next from 3am to 11am. Even those who work shifts don't have that chaotic a schedule! We already have some built in routines, whether we recognize them as that or not. For example, most of us go to bed at approximately the same time every day, and wake up at about the same time. Meal times are approximately the same each day. We have office hours. If we are in school, we have the scheduled class times. Driving a car has become routine. So has brushing your teeth. If you want to fit in exercise, you have to schedule it, and if you schedule it in as a regular activity (like a scheduled class), you might actually do it! Where else can you create a routine?

93

Schedule a regular date night with your spouse/significant other (or social time if you are single)

Let's face it, in the constant press of never ending things to do, projects to complete, errands to run, calls to make, meals to plan, etc., etc., etc., it is far too easy to drop out those relationships that are most important to us. So, before you lay out all the time you are going to be spending on work, errands, etc., mark off time for a date with your spouse or partner or friends. Putting time in the calendar gives you something to look forward to, and ensures that you don't go weeks without any purely social interaction.

94

Do something that scares you

Make time in your schedule for growing and stretching. Get out of your comfort zone. We've all heard that everything you want is outside your comfort zone. You already know what life looks like inside that zone – give yourself a chance to find inspiration. You don't have to jump out of a plane (although that was a blast). Putting yourself in almost any new position, or learning some new skill, will put you in an uncomfortable place for a while. But the results are very worth it!

95
Take time to laugh!

Not only is laughter a great stress buster, it is very good for you! It breaks up whatever pattern you have fallen into, and floods your body with oxygen and feel-good hormones. I keep a folder on my computer of cartoons and jokes that make me laugh, along with links to websites that always make me smile or laugh out loud. When I am feeling stuck, poky, or bogged down, I take a short break and check in with one of those resources. It really does break up whatever had me stuck, and lets me return to the task with more enthusiasm and creativity.

96

Exercise – regularly move your body

We were designed for movement. We have this magnificent machine at our disposal. Spending hours and hours in a chair, at a desk, in front of a computer screen doesn't support this amazing piece of equipment. Get up, take a walk, take a yoga class, go to the cross fit gym, play golf, play soccer, play hopscotch – anything that will get you moving on a regular basis. Why do I include this in a list of things that will give you more time? Well, because staying fit will give you more energy for the rest of your life, and everything that makes up that life. Move.

97
Hire someone to do your bookkeeping

Most of us are just not good at this level of detail, nor do we have the time or patience for all the data entry. You will save yourself hours of time and frustration (and probably a lot of money) by having someone else do your bookkeeping. You will save tons of time at tax time, because everything will already be together and sorted appropriately. Unless, of course, you really love to spend weeks and weeks trying to reconstruct your year in expenses to get your taxes done, or you really love doing detailed financial work late at night, after you finish your job. I would rather turn all those receipts over to someone else to enter, and spend my time either generating more business or playing harder.

98

Checklists are your friend

I don't care how good your memory is. I don't care how often you have done this task. If you really want to save yourself time and get far more done, then take the time to develop and use checklists for everything! The more you can get out of your head, and on to a piece of paper, the more you will actually be able to accomplish, and the less stressed you will be!

99

Use a packing list when traveling

You would think you would remember to repack those shoes before you come home. Until you get home and realize your favorite pair of workout shoes are NOT in the suitcase, because they were UNDER the hotel bed and you never saw them when you were repacking! You would think you would remember to pack your toothbrush and toothpaste – after all you brush your teeth every day. Explain why, then, all hotels have spares for those who forgot? You would think you would remember to bring the charger for your laptop / smart phone / camera / fill in the blank with your favorite electronic device. You would be wrong. You will forget something at some point. If you work from a packing checklist – it is less likely! And then you won't have to spend the time finding a replacement for whatever you forgot.

100

Make up a duplicate toiletries kit, and leave it in your suitcase

I didn't understand why one of my friends always bought two of all of her toiletries and makeup. Even when she explained that with all her travel it just made sense to her to have a duplicate set living in her suitcase all the time, ready to go. Then I started traveling myself. That's when it hit me! What a great idea. Yes, it can cost a little more at the beginning, but it will save so much time and money over the long term. And you can buy travel size versions of almost everything you use on a daily basis.

101

When all else fails

Ask for help! Let's face it, none of us goes it alone. You need a team, you need (and deserve) support. If you have questions or would like to learn more about what Time Triage is all about, go to www.timetriage.com and schedule yourself for a breakthrough productivity session.

About the Author
Terry Monaghan
Time Triage™

Improve Performance | *Produce Results* | *Increase Revenue*

703-829-5097
terry@timetriage.com
www.timetriage.com

Before launching her business, Terry Monaghan (founder and CEO of Time Triage™) invested years being trained and developed in distinctions of planning, time management, leadership, and coaching others to produce results while producing extraordinary results herself. She is well-versed in the theories behind what impacts performance and productivity, but she is far more interested in creating custom solutions for her clients that create a measurable difference today.

With over 30 years of business and entrepreneurial experience, Terry's unique technology has dramatically increased the productivity of Fortune 100 executives, entrepreneurs and professionals. Whether you are a corporate executive or a "solo-preneur," the outcome of Terry's methodology will give you an expanded level of freedom and productivity with results you can measure.

Terry's clients find themselves working on what is most fulfilling and what really matters in moving things forward rather than what they previously thought they "had to do." The things you hoped to get to someday become the things you work on today.

To determine your next steps towards the success you deserve, visit www.timetriage.com to schedule a private Productivity Breakthrough Session.